Open Season

Open Season

Poems by Neva Herrington

Neva Herrington

David Robert Books

To Hua

with best wishes

February 28, 2019

Published by David Robert Books
P.O. Box 541106
Cincinnati, OH 45254-1106

ISBN: 9781625491190
LCCN: 2014959906

Poetry Editor: Kevin Walzer
Business Editor: Lori Jareo

Visit us on the web at www.davidrobertbooks.com

Acknowledgments

The Chariton Review: "A Postcard from Spain,"
"Not Quite Loneliness in Texas," "The Size
of Childhood," "Visit to Jan in Open
Season," "Woodchuck at the Art Colony"
The Comstock Review: "Pumpkin Judging"
Confrontation: "Her BMW"
Connecticut River Review: "Courtship," "Facing
Fort Trumbull with Charles," "Old, My
Father Invented a Machine"
Wind: "Overnight"
The Worcester Review: "Coal-Men Day"

Some of these poems appeared under different
titles.

"Not Quite Loneliness in Texas" is anthologized in
Roth Publishing's *Poem Finder* on the Internet.

The poems in section IV are published in the
chapbook *Her BMW and Other Poems* (Columbus:
Pudding House Publications, 2007), a finalist in the
2006 Pudding House Chapbook Competition.

"Woodchuck at the Art Colony" is published in
Entering The Real World (Amherst: Waverly Press,
2011), an anthology of poems by Fellows at the
Virginia Center for the Creative Arts.

Grateful acknowledgment is made to the Virginia
Center for the Creative Arts for a residence during
which some of these poems were written.

For Barbara Foster Goldman

in grateful memory

Contents

III

IV

I

Visit to Jan in Open Season

Enon Valley, Pennsylvania

All the first evening her dogs barked outside
as if I were a danger in the house
of my friend, a poet, not a farmer,
newcomer to her acres of farmland
under light snow after the long fall drought,

muddying our path through her deer-tracked woods
to a stone shell, cellar of her house torched
by someone the neighbors know but won't name,
both in red hats to keep from getting shot
also on her farm, a children's story:

nine horses, a white duck, two fat-necked geese,
the rooster who froze in a tree and thawed alive,
famous for his night with a skunk in his cage,
the dogs quiet when we left in her truck
for the Amish blacksmith's, along the road

trailer homes, in a gray-lit Amish yard
a clothesline of blue and purple dresses,
winter wheat green-alive in whitened fields
and footprints crossing, telling the hardship
of distance, losing hold in the warming wind.

Old, My Father Invented a Machine

Old, my father invented a machine
to print cloth when he'd lost
to a brand-name conglomerate his small
south Massachusetts mill.

Once I toured his mill, saw patterned fabrics
rise overhead on belts
to a jigging racket and stink of dye,
heard him above the noise

explain how the big boys had bought him out,
but he had a new plan
to make us rich. Afterwards in a room
hung with tools and photos

of stages in the mill's long life, he showed me
his scratchings on paper,
embryo of a machine that could print
more cloth in less time.

In the one-lamp glare on his drawing board
he imagined wheels, gears,
and doctor blades which snarled and failed,
and finally worked the dream

that made his backer rich, my father poor.
He never spoke again
of his namesake, housed in a Southern state,
efficient in glory

and practical cloth. I have a sample
of its first fruit, a length
of pink roses on white cotton, cut clean
from that victory run.

A Family Chair

Sent to me, its inheritor,
the maple, ladder-back armchair
emerges from a five-foot carton
more character than furniture:
the grip of downward-curving arms,
the slightly forward-tilting posture

from metal treads on the back legs,
inclining the chair's occupant
toward family clamor, mine, the day
I asked my father what he lived for,
and as if in the chair he could give
no other answer, he said, "My children."

I once heard in a museum
a Congo people's funeral trumpets,
wooden horns as family icons
to encourage their dead's contented presence.
This chair in its seated silence
makes room for my own to enter.

Courtship

The moon is a smudge of light
over the uneven dark
horizon from end to end
of the small, framed oil painting.

The tree in the right foreground,
unleaving or about to leaf,
inclines toward the moon halfway
up or down the sky as if

to clarify a neutral moment
the moon might yield its way,
no colors but shades
of beige and gray in this work

of a painter later known
for his New England landscapes
inscribed to my mother
with the date above his name,

a birthday and courtship gift
she hung for sixty-eight years
after she said no, after
August 11, 1917.

The Size of Childhood

Bored with safety, sometimes we'd cross
acres of tall grass to a house
unlocked and vacant, sunlight an echo
in rooms with yellow walls, empty
except for a trunk-size box
of fusty-smelling costumes, laid
to rest like the one who wore them:
Richard Mansfield, his fame unknown
to children claiming for ourselves
an abandoned cottage, a tomb for clothes
without bones to rise and accuse
—those outfits in rigid repose,
seen once and not disturbed again—
nor did his widow, old lady
now and then sighted on her cane-paced walks,
interrupt us, leaving each time
what we'd find returning, rooms cleared
of evidence, air no one breathed,
the resident wardrobe not moved.

Harbor

Fishers Island

Promising my father to keep his sailboat
in sight, we set out in the dinghy,
three children under twelve with an island
in mind. The youngest, I sat in the bow,
the first to set foot on the pebbled shore.
The one requirement was to be happy.

We understood (more excited than happy),
ranging the near rocks, seeing the sailboat
color rose in the sunset, that the shore
bound us to the sailboat and the dinghy
with the oars folded like hands in the bow
was more solid than the whole wild island.

The boy among us wanted the island,
led us over a treeless hill, happy
to hear still the waves break far from the bow
of the dinghy, though my father's sailboat
had gone from view. I thought of the dinghy
loosening, washing away from the shore.

The light changed; the sun went under the shore.
Afraid on the fast darkening island,
we raced over the hill to the dinghy,
stumbling on stones, shouting, waving, happy
to see in the calm harbor the sailboat
not moved, an ashen-gray light on its bow.

I took my old place in the bow
as the dinghy turned around from the shore,
aimed on the black, smooth water for the sailboat.
Once or twice I glanced back at the island,
the seaweed strewn shore, the far trees, happy
to leave whatever reached out for the dinghy.

My smiling father welcomed the dinghy,
crouched at the edge of the sailboat's bow.
The bows scraped. I held out my hand, happy,
but my feet stayed in the dinghy. The shore
at my back, I went down like an island
under water that floated the sailboat.

From my father's bow I studied the shore,
the tethered, empty dinghy, the island
by itself, happy, as required, in the sailboat.

Lighthouse Watch

Daylight disclosed the distance the lighthouse
light brought near: three whites and a red
I could see from my pillow, signaling me
—awake late on a summer night—
to the window one more time in the spell
of its rhythm like a dance step to join,
not missing a beat, no land, no water
between us, that unhindered darkness
I had to make sure of again
and again, afraid I'd get caught
out of bed, a child not in place
in a house so quiet I once heard
pages of a book open on the floor
riffled by a breeze from nowhere.

Coal-Men Day

No one alive now can tell you
how often they came, canvas bags
slung from humped shoulders,
a procession of two or three
back and forth as we huddled near
our cellar window walls to watch
the coal lowered and poured down chutes
into two rooms at the dark end

of the longest, darkest cellar
any one of us knew. Rainy
days when we bicycled around
the metal ceiling poles, we stayed
close to the other end: outside door,
washtubs, clotheslines, ironing board,
the earth-smelling preserve closet,
hardly ever riding the slope

to the furnace pit and the coal banks
under the eerie-pale windows.
But once there we lingered to scare
ourselves with the inward-licked flame
of the coal burner, the heaped black
hulks in adjoining stalls forcing
us to attend to their silence
until the last moment of danger

chased us shrieking up the incline
through tunnels of hanging laundry
to the foot of the kitchen stairs
near the door to the jelly jars,
the clove-studded, pickled-brown fruit
on shelves as high as the ceiling
that shook now and then with footsteps
far from the tracks of the coal-men.

Leaf Burial

This November the leaf-blowers scour
the apartment grounds, flurries blown
in a roar of machine wind to mounds
in the parking lots the size of the pile
a gang of us, none older than ten,
raked up that fall in a neighborhood field,
burying two-year old Peter
deeper as he thrashed to breathe only days
before we saw the sign on his front door,
the polio quarantine, and believed—
for years believed—our burying him
had done it, no matter what people said,
his leg brace, his skipping limp, with us
from the day we buried him in the leaves.

Winter Thaw

The crows are standing on the lake
with their usual arrogance,
not so surefooted as the gulls
on the opportunity of thin ice.

Fat as hens, they strut and pick
the puckering ice for windfalls
at the edge of the commotion
stirring the enlarging water,

Mallards and Canada geese
roughhousing in February.
That wing-flaring, bugling goose
requires this courtship temperature.

Ecology

A four-wheeled, rattling orange machine
with a pulsating green plastic hose
and a tin attachment like a stovepipe
drained a three-acre neighborhood lake
to save two bird-scoured islands,

their fibrous undersides exposed
in a mud field of assorted crimes:
shopping carts, bicycle parts, traffic cones,
and dimly disclosed et cetera.
I half expected skeletons.

Geese cancelled arrivals—the county
came for the goose with the dragging wing—
ducks took chances, swam rain pools, dodged
the bulldozer, camped on the latest
heaped-up rubble, ate on their own

before the lady with the sack
of grain returned to the risen lake,
the pump gone, the islands buttressed
with wire-caged rocks, overhead
favorable to flights resumed.

Arthur, a Memoir

Afterwards two friends called
with chicken soup. They spoke
of the deaths of their elderly pets
by euthanasia. I described
my sudden decision at the sight

of that much blood from tumors
inoperable from the start.
I mentioned the strange cough
since summer, the arthritis,
the epilepsy, the heart murmur.

But the day Arthur died,
he walked around the lake,
stopping as usual
for deep investigations,
making himself a stone

as I tried to pull on, and ate
with gusto the slice of pizza
I baked for his last meal
and had a happy expression
looking over my shoulder

in the car and didn't object
to the vet's table but sat
expectantly as if he agreed.
The first needle didn't work.
At the second, he cried out,

in his eyes a look. He knew.
His weight in my arms,
I heard a sound in his throat.
The vet placed the stethoscope.
"He's gone," he said.

So much like a person,
friends would say. The way
I talked about him
at work some people thought
a beagle was my husband.

He slept in my bed,
preferred vegetables and Mozart.
He might have died in his sleep
naturally as we all wish,
companion to his secret pain.

Opera Heart

Alone with the set, I listen
to the live-on-TV audience
scuttling coughs for the curtain rise
on the Met stage, there with you once

on an overdue honeymoon
at the Saturday matinee,
dressed in our best—a lady
asking if we were from the west—

for Verdi's *Don Carlos,* captives
bound to the beat of the auto-da-fé,
heart-stir for our own duet
to outlast error on a grand scale.

Years without you, tonight a nun,
Puccini's *Suor Angelica,*
her madness forgiven, taken
to Heaven, could bring the house down.

Notes from a High School English Class

Moments before
the end of class bell
felt the diamond

absent from my ring,
pledge to a marriage
lately mourned,

informed my students,
heartbreak trained
in Russian Lit,

Tatiana's and Masha's
current with their own
(one writing once

on the blackboard: *Someone
really yours
will come back to you*),

found on my desk
their tribute in bits
of broken glass,

on the floor of my house
the diamond by then
no longer looked for,

not a sign or
a symbol for literature,
a diamond's story.

At the Lyceum

In time for the end of Mozart,
first on the afternoon program
of a rising local star, I take
the last chair on the front row
curving behind the pianist now

at work on Schumann. Her pink back
shows through white voile and lace. Her arms
in puffs and bows shake with the plunge
and race of her fingers. I face
a window, tall and curtainless,

overlooking a parking lot
in foggy twilight. Indoors notes
grind and fly, the audience near
the piano leaning to watch
the accurate strikes. Darkening

outside presents the concert room
in the window glass—the small crowd
and in the rear a candlelit
table of punch and cakes and fruit—
the streetlights early in fall dusk

with the light on the building's roof
opposite, the lights in alleys
and over doorways, the shelter's entrance
for the line each evening gathered
in the hour of her finale chords.

Overnight

The train coach lights go out.
Strangers sleep side by side
as in a giant nursery,

while cities cross faces
like flashlights checking.
Low to the earth the moon

races backwards. I sleep,
wake up to the shine
of rain on the window,

the station unannounced,
a hushed exodus
from the nighttime household.

II

Pumpkin Judging

For Nathaniel

The children came with pumpkins to carve
before dark and the judging, each child
alone with a knife and the deadline dark
and a pumpkin who could be anyone.

Even the late ones finished in time
for the performance, the house lights off,
the better to see the assembly
crossing the black lawn. What could we make

of twenty-six candlelit faces,
all personalities, none alike?
Whatever the style of mouth and eyes,
holes or slits or crescents, whatever

patterns on cheeks, on chins, on foreheads,
whatever adorned the pumpkin flesh
(a pepper tongue, a pirate's nose ring
and every kind of hat), we judges

couldn't agree on best or worst,
judged the winner joined twin pumpkins
with no ornament to distract us
from its two-headed, double gaze.

A Postcard from Spain

For Rodger

This postcard survived a box of letters
kept too long in a damp cellar, postmarked
29 July '68, the scene
(named in the top, left-hand corner above
your *Dearest*): Toledo, a partial view,
a white-foamed river, a narrow shore, a pool
mirroring a stone house, a zigzag road
uphill in rock past bulwark walls to dark
green groves, milky blue sky, the palace where
you wrote you went because it was Sunday.

I don't remember the card or the trip
when you still signed openly to the world
All my love. The address tells me we lived
then in our last house, a pomegranate tree
in the yard and at our bedroom window
the gardenia bush of florist-perfect blooms.
One night you brought home a guest, a stranger
from the North, lighted the driveway for him
to see the gardenia bush in flower.
You filled at least a dozen plastic bags,

shaking water over the limp petals.
Hands full, he left us, astonished at joy
so suddenly in that house. Past divorce,
your death, why does that moment seem sent now
as this postcard once, specific as your
news of the weather in Spain: *like Texas*
but drier and without air-conditioning?
The spires on the palace turrets thin out
to needle points in the sunlit, clear air.
I wonder how far you walked in that heat.

Not Quite Loneliness in Texas

Three months here in a rented house
where former tenants left only
nail holes in doors and papered walls
and one his name on the mailbox:
Fabergé, I watch a backyard,
winter bleached, bird shadows crossing.

The blue jays, the finches make plans,
not wishes; a jay hammers the ground,
finches change places on a branch,
indifferent to past occupants.
Fabergé's name has outlasted
two rounds of tenants. He lived alone,

died somewhere in these rooms. Shy, proud
of his name (not the perfume company
the landlord says he emphasized),
descendant of artists to the Tsar,
professor, famous in his own right,
he talked to himself in Russian.

Inventor of an apparatus
for clocking traffic in a beehive,
a scale to weigh butterfly wings,
year after year he burned dinners
on our terrible stove while birds
seized and let go an empty yard.

Elsewhere

Mornings like this one my open
window travels for dialogue

in Texas sunrise turning mauve
the dusk cones on a tree resembling

a tree I opened my window
in a Dublin hotel to touch,

the flowers reminding me then
of lilacs at home years ago

in New England—their full-flower
give in my hands—the Irish tree

hailing me, nudging a casement
wide to dun–colored, foreign roofs.

Fort Sam Houston: 713 W

Looking for the cemetery,
lost awhile, we parked where I thought
I remembered the place sixteen
years ago, raw for a new grave,
taps and the chaplain's voice, the flag
to take home, the bulldozer not
interrupted, now a harvest
of headstones in all directions,
Sunday silent. I headed west,

my son and daughter-in-law east
among the numbered thousands there
in alphabet convocations,
reading the names of the war dead,
the long-lived dead, spouses, children
buried near, the sun going down
too fast over the grass, over
the dead. I turned around: no one,
our lone car in the empty road,

and ran, calling out my son's name,
his living name frightening me
in the hush of indifferent graves.
Had the car hidden them? I saw
their undivided look, her tears
for a man she had never met
as they stood where they'd found him,
in my son's gaze a day brought back
with the years his father couldn't know.

Vocations

For Anne

My daughter whose garden
this is plants flowers
on her patio,

whatever will thrive
in containers of wood
or terra-cotta.

I'm the guest in a chair
by the swimming pool
a small pool vacuum

tirelessly cleans,
traveling the walls
for remnants of leaves,

surfacing its hose
with a swinging flip
to the heated air

then down to renew
the entire depths.
We go with what we do.

Southwest Move

In Illinois the rattly Nash, bought new
for a fresh start in Texas, rode the rim

of a wheel-deep ditch on two-lane asphalt,
oil wells beyond, grazing mouths in rhythm.

Numb from so much scenery we didn't know,
we four—father, mother, teenage daughters—

had no comment for the Mississippi,
promised as a bonus along the way,

the father, hands wrung from too long steering,
the daughters rigid with distance, and I,

seeing a river had kept its promise,
hoping ever after could do the same.

Gun Club

Not Connecticut under the trees,
though the look my daughter and I
exchanged went back to once home
—the lake there too overgrown to swim—
from where we sat beside water

floating a raft on its black depths
at a table in Texas shade,
gunfire from the shooting range
no hindrance to a reminder
of happiness without effort.

But when the lake shrank, filled in
to make more room for the shooters
and less for the waterborne snakes,
the swim to the raft scarier,
we knew more surely where we were.

Marker

Lake Texoma

Returning alone
to the swimming beach
where orange markers

like sealed barrels
hooked at each end
kept the speedboats out,

not one of the realists
in their swimming belts,
trusting what danger

I could make of water
with orange limits,
I swam to a marker,

dangling, faced
the length of the lake
without a swimmer,

looked back to where
I used to see you
close to the shore

touching bottom,
water the one
distance between us.

A Property for Sale

The sign not removed from the chain-link fence
International Montessori House for Children
enclosing a dirt yard, sun whitened
in the winter noon, you might assume
the twin, weathered-pale jungle gyms,
the two-story beige stucco house
a prefab hut on either side,
doves on the patchy roof, in wait
for vanishing choreographies, not
realtors on the flagstones with clients,
wing flutter at a dormer window
mistaken for movement behind the glass.

III

Tulips

This April municipal
gardeners provide tulips,
unforeseen exuberance
at street corners as if wrought
overnight by the Lord God,

not the tulips my father
imagined one October—
ordering bulbs his death day—
but at this intersection
in the red and white hundreds,

not tulips children (two mine)
waved singing in procession
before the neighbor's phone call:
her tulips all picked! Stolen!
And I could say only: "Yes."

Lynchburg Economy

In its bicentennial year,
I moved to a city
arranged on a hill
—mortality at a glance—

a history worth flags
on the river bridge,
plantings for a downtown
of stores moved on,

a monument staircase
honoring wars,
a landing for each
and the local dead,

at the top a statue
of the Southern soldier,
a park for roses,
their upkeep endowed,

from one bush an essence
too strong to doubt
a fragrance perpetual
as memorial stone.

Summer of the Horse

A newcomer where
I knew no one,
I lived next door
to a horse farm.

At the border fence
I would meet the horse,
alert to my arrival
with an apple to offer,

absent one day
and every day after
not there to confirm me
looked for and known.

Crows at Sweet Briar

The month a bullet killed him,
mad from solitude, poor diet—
If only the soup were thicker,
he wrote to his brother Theo—

van Gogh painted a field with crows,
a dead-end path through a wall of wheat,
his crows heading out to a sky
breaking them back to him, their din

I would guess like what I hear
from trees beyond acres of farm
and nearer, the school's playing field:
white goal posts, red pennants flying,

lighted by a late September
afternoon sun, impersonal
as the far-off flicker of crows
let loose to their own horizons.

Eternal Sleep

In Maureen McCabe's *Eternal Sleep,*
an 8 x 14 inches box montage,
the swirling shapes in black and gray

—a photo of an angel sculpture
and one of a woman outstretched,
head fallen back, interwoven—

recall the pattern on the walls
of the passage grave on Hag's Hill
in Ireland where I watched her

lay sheets of paper over the stone
to rub to life. In this piece, a break
in the overall design shows

a young girl's face, her eyes closed,
a pink rose in her yellow hair
and three at her throat as if just placed there

like the spiral figures she brought forth
in that burial-chamber cell
for the company in eternal sleep.

Pool

A winter sun crosses
the empty concrete deck.

Glitter ribbons the rim
of the sunken waterline.

The swimmers, the lifeguards
on their angled perches,

the infirmary of bodies
in the rows of white deck chairs—

these disappeared—only
a season displaces

from what looks so plainly theirs,
sunning a live vacancy.

Cranes

David Ignatow
"A Dialogue"

Far up the morning sky, two cranes
are reaching for windows not yet
in place or the walls to hold them,

on one crane the contractor's name,
a little box house, a wheeled cart,
a machine-run balancing act

to provision acres of footholds,
my friend's in her high-rise warehouse
for the aged, walking corridors

of locked doors, her windows lookouts
for rescue, her falling flight aimed
as the slow, purposeful lifting of cranes.

Barbara's Amber

Chemotherapy
over and failed,
in a blue turban,
she has put on amber
for me, her friend,

ring and pendant,
petal layered,
collector of amber
in the years of her illness,
more than ornament:

face of a world
in flow, she wrote
in a poem, life
to show in the polished light
of amber hours.

February Sideshow

Midmorning the crepe myrtle,
at sunrise a squirrel's highway

past my window to the roof,
a dove pair's real estate,

shakes to the aim of a pole,
cutting hook at the end,

the man in the white bucket
swings to the interior,

snaring and slicing branches,
ragged with summer's remnants,

heaped on the grass strip edging
the apartment parking lot,

the bucket circling, angling
back to the truck the man,

now in the tree, hand to branch
combat, afterward the view

of surgery one story down
in light left standing.

Facing Fort Trumbull with Charles

Never used as a fort, Charles tells me
in his car parked in the visitors' lot
of the state park, newly developed

at a cost of millions and neighborhoods.
He jokes that grass on the fort's roof
was for catching cannon balls, speaks

of the war he knows, artillery
in the Battle of the Bulge: *War
is to lose people, that's what it's for.*

May sunlight like a color wash
calls attention to the fort's façade,
the darkness behind symmetrical

lookout slits in stone Charles praises,
seen rarely before its present use,
featured with lamps, a winding walk,

a river view for the future hotel,
occupants at their windows to watch
traffic in season at the going cost.

New London, 2013

For Anne Banks

Reunion in our hometown
with my sister cancelled
from her hospital bed,

I'm here for what once
together we had known
to keep our date with change.

At my hotel-room window
I search a skyscape of roofs
and spires for reference,

for the seagulls, constant
in their arrivals
and takeoffs, a foothold.

Between the Worshippers
and the Deer

For Philip

One rainy Sunday morning in June
just past a church, parking lot full,
ahead of me a deer, full grown,

crossed a sloping lawn and the road
into the woods. Seconds later its twin
in size followed, my small car right

after over the two-lane asphalt,
the foliage shaken where they'd gone
on the trail of some known, seasonal meal.

Radio

On a hike in the Blue Ridge
with a daughter and son
after years apart,

broadcast voices
from an adjacent hill
startled us to a standstill,

uncertain in our closeness
to a campsite radio,
turned on at our passing by,

hearing the volume lowered,
waving before moving on,
in years thereafter to say:

Remember that radio?
to recover in an instant
a day without casualties.

Watershed

For Dianne

The deadening nature trail
attracted my friend, a scholar

of opposites. Decay means life,
she said. The brochure promised

a midpoint view: mountain ranges,
a river changing direction,

no mention of peacocks, the pair
ahead on our path, deep in woods.

Hushed, we fell into step behind,
in measure with their swinging gait,

till they turned into a thicket,
letting us pass to the lookout.

They met us, just down from that height,
lingering near where we waited,

puzzled by their delay. For us?
They walked forward. We took the way

we'd come, not to follow peacocks
on an unknown descent to the road.

Corn in America

Four uniform ears
in a paper tray,
airtight in plastic wrap,

don't look like shucked ears,
picked within the hour,
while we sisters waited

those World War II summers
for our mother's order
at the old lady's farm,

her homeland Italy,
our enemy in newsreels
of helmet-marching rows,

no harvest in sight like hers,
sweetness held in the mouth
against the news.

IV

Day Off in Danville, Virginia

That hot August noon the crew
laying tar stopped their machines
and left us, my daughter on a pass
from the state hospital and me,
picnicking in a city park.

We ate sandwiches from a cooler
—two workers seriously at lunch!—
hours away from barred doors,
the bag search at the patient entrance,
the therapists' question: *How to live?*

Our boundaries the mall, mill store, museum,
we chose that day the museum tour
with a highlight view of the roped-off room
where Jefferson Davis gave up a war,
afterward in the museum shop

came upon such colors in a painting,
a wall-length meadow extravagance,
more accurate than anywhere seen,
that for a moment even in Danville
nothing could work without us.

A Reading

From time to time she would give me
her hand to read: pale lines, pale palm
like her early pencil drawings,
the still life fruit shy of itself.
That fall after the hospital,
she asked if I saw a difference.

I'm searching, she said of the years
of every loss: work, partner, home,
finally her health. She would wait
all night in her car for the chance
to see the psychic she trusted
to say where good luck might find her.

She doesn't take much time with me.
To look back and see the future
needs no palm reader. Amateur,
I saw no line marked with her choice
for her life in seasons ahead,
the lines as she'd lived them tentative.

Pegasus

With Elizabeth at her window
in cardiac care we could see
the hospital chopper Pegasus
four stories down land with its cargo
of hurt-alive bodies like hers
the night she died, spoke to the dead,

muffled in tubes, bruised with rescue,
attendants at her side, her life
itself conferring distinction
she had no idea of that week
in intensive care, lost to our
signals, and when she could hear us,

she repeated the word *earring,*
somehow knowing the violence
that had brought her back four times from death
had cost her an earring, yet she
couldn't recognize her brother
(thought he was her dentist), couldn't

recall how she made up her eyes
while her screen showed her heart failing
or the two-hour ambulance ride
to another hospital for tests,
her ailment not rare for a woman
her age with her habits, her hardships:

Prinzmetal's Angina or how
she searched for cigarettes, just one
of which, doctors warned, could kill her,
out of bed trailing connections,
reading over and over what
I wrote explaining her whereabouts

and why; then finally unhooked
from her guardian machines, in her robe,
she smoked outside the main entrance
the first cigarette of her life
as a sequel to death, familiar
enough to convince her she lived.

Labor Day Sonnet

In the Community Services house,
lent for her recovery with neighbors
James, hearing voices, Tom, bipolar, Dennis
at her door all hours for cigarettes,
his stereo loud as a live concert,
more counselor than patient, out of place
there as her furniture out of storage
after three homeless years, that '94
Labor Day, food stamps spent for a hot dog
cookout, she invited the neighborhood
whose labor was living, their turnout more
than her provisions, her kitchen cupboard
emptied of all but one paprika can,
on a desolate shelf a gift left over.

Her BMW

Fredericksburg, Virginia

The mechanic who bought her '83
BMW has promised to make
those repairs she intended: peeling paint
sanded, dents hammered out, body restored
to its original dark blue, leaks sealed,
tattered insides, smoky as a tavern,
and the broken right side-view mirror replaced,
its history since she owned it disappeared.

In six years, 100,000 miles driven
from one home lost to another, the car
ran on minimal attention, broke down
only in sight of help and cash, a roof
any night at the side of the road,
once almost her heart-attack deathbed, parked
at a 7-Eleven. A store clerk,
two paramedics happening by, saved her life.

Deliverance car: down a mountain's edge
in sheet rain, on the road east she followed west,
luxury other homeless couldn't forgive,
an address in itself, her very home,
that November night in the lot outside
her apartment where she lay murdered—
her killer unknown—and just this mileage
to tell exactly how far she had come.

Pinwheel

At Sammy T's where we'd had lunch
two months before your burial
tomorrow, watching a pinwheel

in a window across the street
spinning Christmas, recalling how
you said here: "We had a nice time,"

I wonder if you meant just that day
I drove two hours to see you
after a dream, your eyes closed, ivy

on your forehead, sure you'd told me
in your way you wouldn't live long,
or if you summed up all the times

turning us alike toward the world
in consolations short of joy,
new to this town so soon finding

the two pastels we would go back
over and over to see if
still for sale in the shop window,

agreeing to ask the artist
to hold them for us. Together
we could pay for them by Christmas.

Seasons for Elizabeth (1948-1994)

I *Shelter*

Released from the state hospital
with twenty dollars, no address,
you made up a place to go

to satisfy the staff, drove off
in a battered BMW,
caged like you five months, still running.

Winter nights at the shelter, back
from waitressing at a highway restaurant,
you could hear children

and trains so near you might have stalled
on the tracks, yourself remaining
in always a body you had to keep.

II *Farm*

This highway south in spring you also saw:
redbud on one side, on the other
thin trees like flower stems, the leafing
in red and green all at the top,
ahead the Blue Ridge Mountains, our
getaway, picnics at overlooks,
the hike to the museum farm.

There in April three trees in a field
looked spiritual to you, later
thickened to too much green. In August
we lingered for the garden of corn
and its well-dressed scarecrow—*Look, Mother!*—
your hand holding the place for me,
at your side then, seeing that harvest.

III *Peach Orchard*

Following signs, we came to no
orchard, no acres of peach trees,

but a stand with peaches for sale,
a patch of close-planted peach trees.

We sat under a canvas canopy.
I ate frozen yogurt (peach,

of course). You lighted a cigarette,
forbidden since your heart attack,

tired of peaches in season,
that rumor of a real orchard.

IV *Pyracantha*

Threaded on fences, massed on hills,
pyracantha brings back its own
orange berries another year.
Knife-edge blue sky pares each cluster.
Your last October you stopped our car
at a public bush for a branch
to take home and show in a jar.

Porch chair turned empty to the sun,
white table without the candle
you burned to keep you company,
look too much themselves in light this hard.
A month before you died you stole
pyracantha, your single stem
burgeoning here in strangers' yards.

Clothing the Dead

Late summer racks of merchandise
on the mall sidewalk, marked down,
catch me on my way somewhere else,
not wanting to single her out
from among those fabric shoulders,
no longer here for the white blouse
she might have grabbed for the bargain.
Impossible not to see her
in that blue-green jumper—arms
thin from meals postponed past hunger,
fingers waving a cigarette—
appraising with me this window
of mannequins dressed for the fall,
a new season, a change of clothes.

Perfume

Whenever her favorite perfume
went on sale, I'd buy a supply

the way I'd stock up on candles
or toilet paper, not luxuries.

Je Reviens, White Shoulders, L'Aimant:
she moved in air identified,

solidarity in a scent
with the world's fragile offerings.

On our last shopping trip, she chose
a bottle of something nameless,

cheap, brightly colored, from a bin,
bargain enough, though not her kind,

that too strong, too sweet scent urgent
for notice apart from her.

Benches

Placed-for-the-view benches
on the condominium grounds
seat no one most of the time,

empty for the after-work
tennis match on the lighted court,
for the stream where the surface moves

with circles of unseen life,
passed up by runners, walkers
for health like me, this morning

inviting my daughter, in life,
lover of intervals benches
provide. Losing her eyeglasses

somewhere she couldn't remember,
she stopped searching, sure of their loss,
found them on her bench with a view.

Sun

No such sun as here,
late through my western window,
reached us summer afternoons
hiking mountain woods,
cocooned in a leaf-locked shade.

No sunset-colored detail
in a searchlight focus
liberated our notice
from any landmark other
than our own sunless weather.

Nowhere shadowed blazed out then
like the cave in our last park,
resembling the one we would pass,
dim as ourselves that summer.
Two years and miles from those walks,

she, with ten days to live,
signaled her recognition
of a place recovered, over
us the fall leaves like fires lit
before giving way to the sun.

Namesake

The leaves of the geranium I named
for her are curled up like her hands
the night of her heart attack, a sign,
the nurse said, she was giving up.
But she let death go that time.

So this geranium, four years ago
all leaves when I invoked
her spirit on its behalf, scared
if nothing changed, eternity
might also have its boundaries,

shortly flowered in such abundance
friends noticed. Now these stiffened stems
look past treatment as usual,
at risk to prove her here in a flower
performing for joy in the world.

Virginia Center
for the Creative Arts, 2000

I *Trains*

Fields here are the color
and height I remember
from years ago,
this morning early
after rain
each curving blade
beaded alike,

tracks in the gully
(the double track
becoming one
at the signal light)
still active with trains
I run to the bridge
to catch underneath

and make a wish,
this time for words
exact as a shower
overnight on a field
for a daughter's lifelong
losses she met
in a word: *setback.*

75

And just that word
to cover her absence,
her death no more
than a train's wait
for a track to clear,
this trail of words
a caboose waving?

II *Sylvia Moves Out*

A friend since the afternoon
I met her unloading branches
for her sculptures, vine balls
in sizes various as planets,
packed up now in her truck bed,
Sylvia says she'll write, wants to hear
more about my child murdered,

whose spirit revived a geranium,
who could find me anywhere,
who would grow plants in corners
of rooms like this studio
with its smell of a fresh paint
future as if there were no
such thing as temporary.

III *Woodchuck*

At dinner someone mentions a sighting,
a resident appearing too often
to discredit, not familiar, bigger
than a rat, chestnut-brown, and slow moving.
City folk, most of us, we guess. *Hedgehog?*
Groundhog? Finally *woodchuck* satisfies.

So I'm prepared several days later
for the stir in the field near my door,
the body lumbering through sunlit brush,
a celebrity to transients surprised
by a creature requiring no other
than ground-level horizons, at home here.

Oregon Coast

From a surf too cold for swimmers
this stone, pecan-size and color,
pocked and yellow-streaked— volcanic
action with a dash of sulfur—
carries its story like memory weathered,

what the lady selling coffee
in the Blue Ridge Mountains store
saw in my daughter's face: *Honey,*
you look like you've come a long way,
years past her death as far as here.

If You Were Egyptian

If instead of ashes
in a twentieth-century urn,

you were Egyptian
in the time of pharaohs,

you might turn up
in a resin mask,

discoveries unwound
in your many wrappings:

a brass ashtray,
copper skillet,

a miniature vase
of blue pottery,

that one belonging
you never let go:

the matriarch icon,
her body a household,

candle in a jar,
your face in firelight

at the small hearth
of its flame, you

here in the witness,
the secrecy of things.

CPSIA information can be obtained
at www.ICGtesting.com
Printed in the USA
FFOW03n0010241215
19655FF